MASTERING TAMBOUI

CW01507699

A Comprehensive Guide to
Craft with different techniques and projects

KARY MCCDONALD

Copyright@2024

TABLE OF CONTENTS

Chapter 1

TAMBOUR BEADING

The 18th-century French art of tambour beading is one of the oldest forms of needlework. It is a traditional embroidery technique. Making elaborate beadwork on fabric is the goal of this technique, which requires a unique tambour hook that looks like a small crochet hook. Using a hook to thread beads onto fabric in a chain-like method, different patterns and motifs can be created by stretching the fabric taut in a frame.

Couture clothing, bridal attire, accessories, and even home décor items can be adorned with exquisite and intricate embroidery using tambour beading. Mastering the technique takes time and effort, but the payoff is worth it because it can elevate any job with its beautiful, glamorous effects.

With tambourine beading, artists can play around with a wide variety of threads, fabrics, and beads to create one-of-a-kind creations. Tambourine beading can be anything from a delicate accent to a show-stopping focal point, depending on the complexity of the pattern.

The adaptability of tambour beading is a plus. This versatile embellishment is perfect for a wide range of projects because it may be used on silk, tulle, velvet, and even leather. Tabouring may take your designs to the next level, whether you're adorning a bridal gown with glittering beads, a cocktail dress with intricate patterns, or a clutch or purse with embellishments.

Tambourine beading has developed from its origins in conventional needlework methods to integrate contemporary materials and styles. Craftspeople nowadays frequently combine tambour beadwork with other embroidery techniques, such silk shading, goldwork, or stumpwork, to produce one-of-a-kind and inventive items.

Tambourine beading is an enjoyable and

satisfying creative path for anybody, from experienced embroiderers seeking to enhance their technique to novices wanting to learn something new. The intricate beauty of tambour beading may be yours to create with a little perseverance, practice, and love of beadwork.

Tambour bead

Traditional tambour beading embroidery requires a specific instrument called a tambour bead, sometimes called a tambour hook. Its thin, pointed tip and tiny hook give it the appearance of a crochet hook. The tambour hook is a tool for producing elaborate beading designs by picking up beads and stitching them onto fabric in a chain-like fashion. It is crucial for becoming an expert tambour beader since it enables the regulated and accurate placing of beads.

ADVANTAGES

The capacity to quickly and precisely produce elaborate beadwork is a benefit of tambour beading. Beads may be picked up and attached to fabric in a continuous manner with ease using the tambour hook, which results in stitches that are smooth and uniform. Because it is so much faster than other bead embroidery techniques, tambour beading is perfect for tasks that call for elaborate designs or a lot of beadwork.

Furthermore, tambour beading provides a great deal of leeway in terms of design options. By experimenting with various shapes, sizes, and colors of beads, artisans can fashion a vast array of patterns, motifs, and textures. Because of its adaptability, the possibilities for personalization are practically limitless, whether one is working with clothing, accessories, or home décor.

Additionally, tambour beading exudes an air of professionalism and refinement. An elevated project's aesthetic can be achieved by meticulous attention to detail, such as straight stitches and snug beadwork. Because of this, tambour beading is used for high-end uses like as couture, bridal attire, and other areas that demand meticulous craftsmanship.

Tambor beading is a popular choice among craftsmen and designers who want to add beautiful beadwork to their projects because of its efficiency, variety, and professional finish.

HISTORY OF TAMBOUR BEADING

The art of tambour beading has a long and illustrious history. Its 18th-century French origins and meteoric rise to fame coincide with the Rococo and Baroque eras. It all started with the adornment of robes worn by nobility and royalty with glistening beads and elaborate patterns.

The embroidery frame, which is a wooden hoop or frame stretched with fabric, is called a "tambour" in the procedure. French for "drum," the word "tambour" describes the tight surface of the frame that looks like a drumhead.

In the nineteenth century, tambour beading was all the rage, especially during the Victorian era when ornate beadwork was all the rage as a fashion accessory. Accessory items like handbags and fans, as well as formal dresses and shawls, were adorned with tambour beading.

In the early 1900s, when simpler forms were all the rage, tambour beading went out of style. But in the middle of the twentieth century, when interest in old crafts and couture techniques came back, it saw a renaissance.

Traditional and modern tambour beading are both carried on by artists and designers all around the globe today. Its exquisite beadwork adorns bridal gowns, haute couture pieces, accessories, and even home decor textiles.

Incorporating new materials, styles, and technology, contemporary artisans have kept this centuries-old trade of tambour beading current and vibrant in the contemporary fashion and textile sectors, although the core technique remains essentially untouched.

Chapter 2

TOOLS AND MATERIALS

There are a few necessities for tambour beading practice. To kick things off, here is a simple list:

1. Tambour Hook: The tambour hook, which looks like a tiny crochet hook but has a pointier tip and a smaller hook at the end, is the main tool for tambour beading. It's a tool for stitching beads onto fabric.
2. Embroidery Frame: A hoop or frame made of wood or plastic that is used for embroidery to pull the fabric taut while you work. Because of this, beading is easy and tension is maintained consistently.
3. Fabric: Select a material that is ideal for tambour beading, like organza, tulle, silk, or lightweight cotton. To ensure the beads and stitches don't fall out, make sure the fabric is securely woven.
4. Beads: Gather a variety of beads in sizes, shapes, and colors to create your masterpiece. Though traditional seed beads are most often utilized, different materials such as pearls, sequins, or crystals can also be experimented with.
5. Thread for beading: Use a thin, strong thread made for beadwork, like polyester or nylon. Be sure the thread complements the fabric and beads.
6. Beading Wax: Applying a coating of beading wax or conditioner to your thread is an optional step that will make it smoother and simpler to manipulate.

Tangling and fraying can be avoided with this method.

7. Scissors: For thread cutting and fabric trimming, sharp stitching scissors are a must-have.

8. Tools for transferring designs: You might use tracing paper or water-soluble markers to transfer the design to the cloth, but this will depend on your design.

9. Lighting and magnification: When working with small beads or fine details, it can be helpful to have good lighting and magnification while doing detailed beadwork.

10. If you want to stitch without using your hands, an embroidered stand or holder can be helpful. This way, you can concentrate on guiding the tambour hook.

When you start your tambour beading journey with these materials, you'll have all you need to create stunning beaded designs on cloth. You may always experiment with new methods and embellishments to make your creations even more special as you get more experience.

REQUIRED OFFICE SPACE

For efficient tambour beading practice, it is vital to create a comfortable environment. Some suggestions for organizing your work area are as follows:

1. Select a Level, Stable Surface: Sit down at a desk or table that has a level, stable surface. This will ensure that your embroidery frame doesn't move about while you stitch by providing a solid base.
2. Good Lighting: Make sure your work area is well-lit so you can see what you're doing without straining your eyes. If you can't get enough natural light where you work, a powerful desk lamp or adjustable lights will do the trick.
3. Comfortable Seating: Thirdly, make sure you're sitting comfortably with adequate back support so you can keep your posture straight as you work. Because tambour beading is a labor-intensive craft, you should wear comfortable shoes because you will likely spend long hours at your workspace.
4. Organized Storage: Maintain an organized storage space for all of your equipment, materials, and supplies. Beads, threads, and other accessories

can be kept in order with the use of storage containers, trays, or organizers.

5. Sufficient Room: Give yourself enough of room to work with your embroidery frame and tambour hook. Make sure your work area is free of clutter so you can move around easily and stay focused.

6. Ventilation: To keep yourself and others healthy, make sure your work area has enough ventilation if you're using gases-emitting materials like adhesives, sprays, or paints.

7. An Inspiration Board: To stay motivated and inspired while you work on your projects, consider putting up an inspiration board or wall nearby. You can pin swatches of colors, sketches, and design ideas on it.

8. Noise Control: Work in a peaceful environment to reduce interruptions, particularly when concentrating on detailed beadwork that demands undivided attention.

In order to have a pleasant and fruitful creative experience while immersing yourself in the art of tambour beading, it is important to establish a separate and orderly work area.

BASIC TECHNIQUES

Listed below are the supplies and methods for three different types of tambour beading:

1. **Chain Stitch Beading:**

Materials Needed:

- Fabric (such as silk or tulle)
- Tambour hook
- Beading thread
- Beads of your choice
- Embroidery frame
- Scissors

Step-by-Step:

1. Make sure the fabric is tautly stretched over the embroidery frame.

2. Knot the end of a strand of beading thread and thread it onto the tambour hook.
3. Insert the hook into the cloth from underneath and bring it to the surface where your design begins.
4. Thread a bead onto the peg.
5. Make a little loop on the surface by inserting the hook back into the fabric just before the starting place.
6. To construct a chain stitch and fasten the bead, pull the thread through the loop.
7. Following your planned pattern or motif, repeat steps 4-6 for every bead in your creation.
8. Knot the thread securely on the bottom of the fabric when you've finished beading.

2. Backstitch Beading:

Materials Needed:

- Fabric
- Tambour hook
- Beading thread
- Beads

- Embroidery frame
- Scissors

Step-by-Step:

1. Stretch the fabric onto the embroidery frame.
2. Thread a length of beading thread onto the tambour hook, tying the end with a knot.
3. Insert the hook from the underside of the fabric, bringing it up to the surface at the starting point of your pattern.
4. Slide a bead onto the hook.
5. Insert the hook back into the fabric slightly behind the starting position, securing the bead in place.
6. Bring the hook up to the surface again, a short distance ahead of the initial bead.
7. To make a row of beads linked by backstitches, slide another bead onto the hook and repeat steps 5-6.
8. Keep stitching in place the beads in this way, following your design.

3. Overlay Beading:

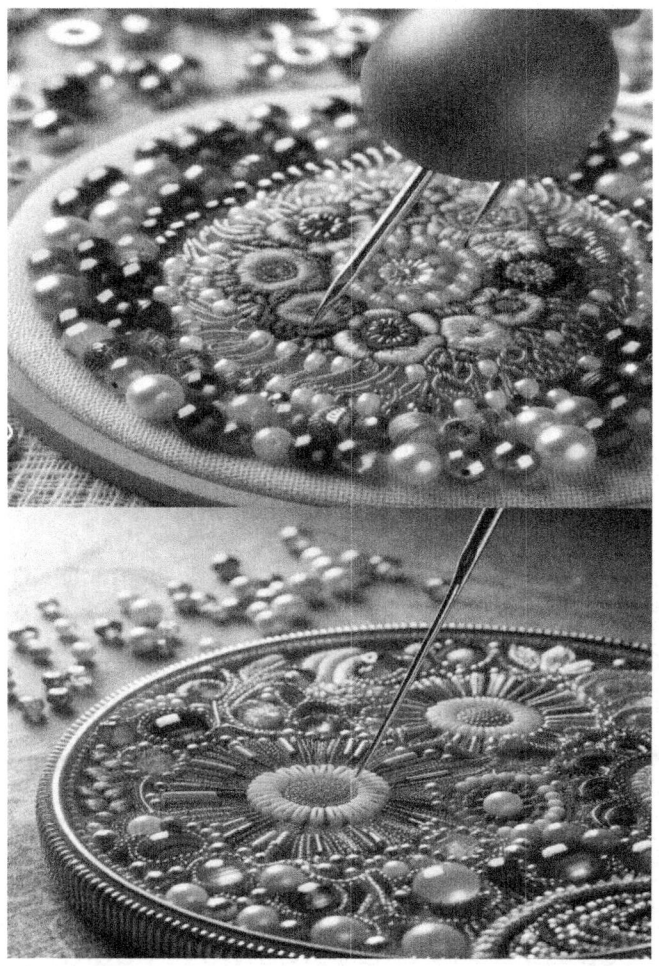

Materials Needed:

- Fabric
- Tambour hook
- Beading thread
- Beads

- Embroidery frame
- Scissors

Step-by-Step:

1. Stretch the fabric onto the embroidery frame.
2. Knot the end of a strand of beading thread and thread it onto the tambour hook.
3. Insert the hook into the cloth from underneath and bring it to the surface where your design begins.
4. Thread a number of beads onto the hook, making sure there are enough to cover the area you wish to bead.
5. Secure the beads in place by inserting the hook back into the fabric little ahead of the beginning position.
6. Raise the hook back up to the surface and place it alongside the initial row of beads.
7. With the fresh row of beads layered on top of the old, slide it onto the hook and repeat steps 5 and 6.
8. Keep going in the same way, adding rows of beads until you've covered the area you want with layers of beads.
   Just to get you started, here are a few basic tambour beading techniques. Try out various stitches, patterns, and bead combinations to make your own one-of-a-kind creations as your skill level rises.

INTERMEDIATE TECHNIQUES

The following are the materials and methods required to complete three intermediate tambour beading projects:

1. **Picot Edge Beading:**

Materials Needed:

- Fabric
- Tambour hook
- Beading thread
- Beads
- Embroidery frame
- Scissors

Step-by-Step:

1. Put the fabric on the embroidery frame by stretching it.
2. Knot the end of a strand of beading thread and thread it onto the tambour hook.
3. Insert the hook into the cloth from underneath and bring it to the surface where your design begins.
4. Thread a bead onto the peg.
5. Return the hook to the cloth just before the beginning point and secure the bead.
6. Return the hook to the surface and place it alongside the initial bead.
7. Continue stitching beads into a row by sliding another bead onto the hook and repeating steps 4-6.
8. After you've knotted the last bead, raise the hook to the surface close to the first bead to make a picot edge.
9. To make a loop, thread a tiny bead onto the hook and thread it through the fabric.

10. To fasten the picot, reinsert the hook into the cloth through the loop.
11. Make any necessary adjustments to the size and spacing of the beads and picots as you continue to add them along the edge of your pattern.

2. **Ruching Beading:**

Materials Needed:

- Fabric
- Tambour hook
- Beading thread
- Beads
- Embroidery frame
- Scissors

Step-by-Step:

1. Lay the cloth out on top of the embroidery frame.
2. Knot the end of a strand of beading thread and thread it onto the tambour hook.
3. Insert the hook into the cloth from underneath and bring it to the surface where your design begins.
4. Thread a bead onto the hook.
5. To secure the bead, insert the hook back into the cloth just before the beginning point.
6. Raise the hook back up to the surface and place it alongside the initial bead.
7. Continue to create a line of beads by sliding another bead onto the hook and repeating steps 4-6.
8. After you've secured each bead, you can make ruching by inserting the hook slightly below the bead.
9. Generously gather the cloth around the bead by gently pulling the thread.

10. Make any necessary adjustments to the spacing and gathers as you continue to add beads and ruching throughout the length of your pattern.

3. Layering Beading:

Materials Needed:

- Fabric
- Tambour hook
- Beading thread
- Beads
- Embroidery frame

- Scissors

Step-by-Step:

1. Lay the cloth out on top of the embroidery frame.
2. Knot the end of a strand of beading thread and thread it onto the tambour hook.
3. Insert the hook into the cloth from underneath and bring it to the surface where your design begins.
4. Thread a bead onto the hook.
5. To secure the bead, insert the hook back into the cloth just before the beginning point.
6. Raise the hook back up to the surface and place it alongside the initial bead.
7. Continue to create a line of beads by sliding another bead onto the hook and repeating steps 4-6.
8. With each row of beads secured, add more rows of beads, slightly offset from each row, by repeating steps 4–7. This will create layers.
9. In order to give your pattern depth and dimension, keep adding layers of beads in this way, modifying their arrangement and spacing.

Beadwork on fabric can take many forms when one masters these intermediate tambour beading techniques. Play around with various bead sizes, colors, and patterns to make elaborate and one-of-a-kind designs.

ADVANCED TECHNIQUES

The following are the supplies and methods for three different types of advanced tambour beading:

1. **Floating Beads**:

Materials Needed:

- Fabric
- Tambour hook
- Beading thread
- Beads (preferably larger or dimensional beads)

- Embroidery frame
- Scissors

Step-by-Step:

1. Put the fabric on the embroidery frame by stretching it.
2. Knot the end of a strand of beading thread and thread it onto the tambour hook.
3. Insert the hook into the cloth from underneath and bring it to the surface where your design begins.
4. Attach a big bead on the hook.
5. Return the hook to the cloth just before the beginning point and secure the bead.
6. Return the hook to the surface and place it alongside the initial bead.
7. To make a row of big beads, slide another big bead onto the hook and repeat steps 4-6.
8. Return the hook to the cloth directly below each large bead after securing it to produce raised beading.
9. Lift the bead just a little bit off the fabric surface by pulling the thread taut.
10.   To add dimension and texture to your design.
11.   Keep adding rows of raised beads in this way, altering the spacing and placement.

2. Layered Embellishments:

Materials Needed:

- Fabric
- Tambour hook
- Beading thread
- Beads (various sizes, shapes, and textures)
- Sequins, crystals, or other embellishments
- Embroidery frame
- Scissors

Step-by-Step:

1. Lay the cloth out on the embroidery frame.
2. Knot the end of a strand of beading thread and thread it onto the tambour hook.

3. Insert the hook into the cloth from underneath and bring it to the surface where your design begins.
4. Fasten a bead onto the hook in any way you like.
5. Stitch or loop the thread around each ornament, such as beads, sequins, or whatever else you choose, to create a layered effect.
6. To add texture and depth to your design, try using various combinations of decorations such as beads and sequins.
7. Keep piling on the embellishments, switching up the shapes, sizes, and textures until you have the effect you want.
8. Secure and evenly distribute each layer of embellishments to the fabric with the tambour hook.

3. **Bullion Stitch Beading:**

Materials Needed:

- Fabric
- Tambour hook
- Beading thread
- Beads (optional, for added embellishment)
- Embroidery frame
- Scissors

Step-by-Step:

1. Lay the cloth out on top of the embroidery frame.
2. Knot the end of a strand of beading thread and thread it onto the tambour hook.

3. Insert the hook into the cloth from underneath and bring it to the surface where your design begins.
4. If you'd like, slide a bead onto the hook. If you're only concerned with the bullion stitch, you can omit this step.
5. Maintain an open loop by twisting the thread multiple times around the hook.
6. Place the hook just in front of the beginning point on the fabric and draw the loop through to create a twisted stitch on the surface.
7. Make more bullion stitches by repeating steps 4-6 and modifying the length and spacing to your liking.
8. Align and securely attach each bullion stitch to the fabric with the tambour hook.

These intricate tambour beading techniques demand a great deal of concentration, persistence, and accuracy, but the end product is often worth the effort. Try your hand at tambour beading with a variety of materials, textures, and designs to see what you can come up with.

Chapter 3

SOLUTIONS AND TROUBLESHOOTING

In order to have a pleasant and trouble-free crafting experience, it is helpful to know how to troubleshoot typical tambour beading problems. Some typical issues and how to fix them are as follows:

1. **Thread Tangles or Breaks:**

   - **Cause:** Using a thread that is too long or tangled, or pulling too tightly on the thread.
   - **Solution:** Use shorter lengths of thread to reduce tangling, and avoid pulling too tightly when stitching. Using a beading wax or conditioner can also help strengthen the thread and prevent breakage.

2. **Beads Not Staying in Place:**

   - **Cause:** Insufficient tension in the thread, or using beads that are too heavy for the fabric.
   - **Solution:** Ensure that the fabric is stretched tightly in the embroidery frame to provide adequate tension. Choose beads that are appropriate

for the fabric and use a slightly thicker thread for added support if needed.

3. **Uneven Stitches or Bead Placement:**

   - **Cause:** Inconsistent tension in the thread or improper technique.
   - **Solution:** Practice maintaining a steady tension while stitching, and ensure that the tambour hook is inserted and pulled through the fabric smoothly for each stitch. Take your time and pay attention to detail to achieve even stitches and bead placement.

4. **Fabric Puckering or Distorting:**

   - **Cause:** Pulling the thread too tightly or stitching with too much tension.
   - **Solution:** Use a lighter touch when stitching to avoid pulling the fabric too tightly. If the fabric is prone to puckering, consider using a stabilizer or backing fabric to provide additional support.

5. **Difficulty Manipulating the Tambour Hook:**

   - **Cause:** Inexperience or lack of familiarity with the tambour hook technique.

- **Solution:** Practice using the tambour hook on scrap fabric before starting your project to become more comfortable with the technique. Experiment with different angles and grips to find what works best for you.

6. **Difficulty Following a Pattern:**

   - **Cause:** Unclear or complex patterns, or lack of experience with pattern reading.
   - **Solution:** Start with simple patterns and gradually work your way up to more complex designs as you gain experience. Break down the pattern into smaller sections and focus on one at a time, referring to any accompanying diagrams or instructions for clarity.

You can improve your tambour beading abilities and have a more pleasant making experience by figuring out and fixing these typical problems. Always keep in mind that the secret to becoming an expert at this complex art form is to practice and be patient.

BEGINNER-FRIENDLY PROJECTS

Here are ten tambour beading projects that are perfect for beginners, along with the materials you'll need for each:

1. **Beaded Bookmark**:

Materials Needed:
- Fabric (cotton or linen)
- Tambour hook
- Beading thread
- Seed beads
- Embroidery hoop
- Scissors

Step-by-Step:

1. Measure the size of the fabric you want to use as a bookmark and cut it to fit.
2. To maintain a taut cloth, stretch it onto an embroidery hoop.

3. Use beading thread to thread the tambour hook and secure the end with a knot.
4. Thread the hook through the fabric starting from the bottom and bring it to the top.
5. Stitch a basic pattern or design onto the fabric using seed beads that you have slipped onto the hook.
6. Keep adding beads until the area you want to cover is covered.
7. Trim any surplus thread and knot it firmly on the underside of the fabric.

2. **Beaded Hair Clip:**

Materials Needed:

- Fabric (felt or leather)
- Tambour hook
- Beading thread
- Seed beads or small beads
- Hair clip or barrette
- Glue (optional)
- Scissors

Step-by-Step:

1. Measure and cut the fabric so it will fit the hair clip.
2. Put the cloth through its paces on an embroidery hoop.
3. Use beading thread to thread the tambour hook and secure the end with a knot.
4. Thread the hook through the fabric starting from the bottom and bring it to the top.
5. Make a design or pattern on the fabric by stitching seed beads that you have slipped onto the hook.
6. Keep adding beads until the fabric is covered.
7. After finishing the beading, attach the cloth to the hair clip using adhesive and allow it to dry.
8. Then, trim the hair clip's edges to remove any extra fabric.

3. **Greeting Card with Beads**:

Materials Needed:

- Cardstock or heavy paper
- Tambour hook
- Beading thread
- Seed beads or small beads
- Glue
- Scissors

Step-by-Step:

1. Create a greeting card by folding heavy paper or cardstock in half.
2. Use beading thread to thread the tambour hook and secure the end with a knot.

3. Poke a hole in the card from underneath and drag the hook through to the top.
4. Bring the hook up to speed, then thread the seed beads onto the card in a pattern or design.
5. Keep stringing beads onto the card until the front is covered.
6. Once the beading is finished, glue any threads that are loose to the back of the card.
7. Add more beadwork to the envelope if you like, then write your message inside the card.

4. **Beaded Keychain:**

Materials Needed:

- Felt or leather

- Tambour hook
- Beading thread
- Seed beads or small beads
- Keychain ring
- Scissors

Step-by-Step:

1. Shape your felt or leather into a keychain shape, like a circle or a heart.
2. Use beading thread to thread the tambour hook and secure the end with a knot.
3. Poke a hole in the fabric at the bottom and thread the hook through to the top.
4. Stitch a pattern or design onto the fabric using seed beads that you have slipped onto the hook.
5. Make sure to cover the fabric shape by continuing to add beads.
6. After finishing the beading, glue or stitch the keychain ring to the top of the shape.
7. Cut off any extra fabric that hangs over the keychain's edges.

5. **Beaded Sachet Bag:**

Materials Needed:

- Fabric (organza or sheer fabric)
- Tambour hook
- Beading thread
- Seed beads or small beads
- Ribbon
- Scissors

Step-by-Step:

1. Make sure both the front and back of the sachet bag are rectangles of fabric.
2. Use beading thread to thread the tambour hook and secure the end with a knot.

3. Thread the hook through one fabric rectangle from the bottom and bring it to the top.
4. Stitch a pattern or design onto the fabric using seed beads that you have slipped onto the hook.
5. Keep adding beads until the fabric is covered.
6. To make the second fabric rectangle, follow steps 3-5 again.
7. After beading both pieces of cloth, lay them together with the beaded sides facing each other.
8. Sew a little hole in the fabric at each edge.
9. Insert the opening of the sachet bag and turn it right side out.
10. Stuff the bag with fragrant beads or potpourri.
11. Sew the clasp closed.
12. Turn the bag into a drawstring by threading a ribbon through the opening and tying it.

6. **Bracelet with Beads**:

Materials Needed:
- Beading wire or stretch cord
- Seed beads or small beads
- Crimp beads (if using beading wire)
- Clasp (if using beading wire)
- Tambour hook
- Beading thread
- Scissors

Step-by-Step:

1. Measure the length of the bracelet you want to make and cut a piece of stretch cord or beading wire to fit.
2. Use beading thread to thread the tambour hook and secure the end with a knot.

3. Thread the hook with seed beads and sew them onto the chain or wire in a pattern.
4. Keep stringing beads onto the wire or rope until it is long enough to cover it.
5. Use crimp beads and a clasp to secure the ends of the beading wire.
6. Cut off any extra wire or thread.
7. Remove any extra length from the ends of the stretch cord and bind them tightly.

7. **Beaded Earrings:**

Materials Needed:

- Earring hooks
- Beading wire or headpins
- Seed beads or small beads
- Crimp beads (if using beading wire)
- Tambour hook
- Beading thread
- Scissors

Step-by-Step:

1. Measure the length of the beading wire or headpin that you want for your earrings and cut it to fit.
2. Use beading thread to thread the tambour hook and secure the end with a knot.
3. Stitch a pattern or design onto the wire or headpin after sliding the seed beads onto the hook.
4. Do not stop adding beads until the entire length of the headpin or wire has been covered.
5. Use crimp beads to secure the ends of the beading wire and attach the earring hooks.
6. Make a loop at the beginning of each beaded segment and connect earring hooks if you're using headpins.
7. Cut off any extra wire or thread.

8. **Napkin Rings with Beads**:

Materials Needed:

- Felt or fabric
- Tambour hook
- Beading thread
- Seed beads or small beads
- Ribbon or elastic cord
- Scissors

Step-by-Step:

1. For the napkin rings, cut fabric or felt strips to the width you like.
2. Use beading thread to thread the tambour hook and secure the end with a knot.
3. Thread the hook through the fabric strip from the bottom and bring it to the top.

4. Stitch a pattern or design onto the fabric using seed beads that you have slipped onto the hook.
5. Until you've covered the entire fabric strip, keep adding beads.
6. After beading is finished, cut the fabric strip into a ring and sew the ends.
7. To make a loop to tie around napkins, attach a length of ribbon or elastic cord to both ends of the napkin ring.

9. **Beaded Brooch:**

Materials Needed:

- Fabric (felt or fabric of choice)
- Tambour hook
- Beading thread
- Seed beads or small beads
- Pin back
- Glue
- Scissors

Step-by-Step:

1. Use fabric or felt to cut out a design, such a flower or a heart, to use as a brooch.
2. Use beading thread to thread the tambour hook and secure the end with a knot.

3. Thread the hook through the fabric starting from the bottom and bring it to the top.
4. Thread the hook with seed beads and sew them onto the fabric in a pattern.
5. If you want to cover the fabric shape, you can keep adding beads.
6. Once you've finished beading, the next step is to glue a pin back into the cloth shape and allow it to dry.
7. When you reach the corners of the brooch, trim off any extra fabric.

10. **Coaster with Beads**:

Materials Needed:
- Felt or fabric
- Tambour hook
- Beading thread

- Seed beads or small beads
- Fabric glue

Step-by-Step:

1. Determine the size of the coaster you want by cutting a square or round piece of fabric or felt.
2. Wind some beaded thread through the tambour hook and tie a knot at the end.
3. Thread the hook through the fabric starting from the bottom and bring it to the top.
4. Stitch seed beads onto fabric in a pattern or design of your choice after sliding them onto the hook. Whether you prefer abstract designs, floral motifs, or geometric patterns, the sky's the limit.
5. Bead the fabric all over until it is covered.
6. Let any extra thread hang on the coaster's reverse side when the beading is finished.
7. If you'd like, you can fix the threads and beads in place by applying fabric glue to the back of the cloth.
8. Before you use the coaster to shield your tables from scalding or freezing beverages, make sure it dries entirely.

Get comfortable with the process and practice fundamental techniques with these beginning tambour beading projects. You can personalize each craft to your preference by experimenting with different colors, bead sizes, and patterns. Enjoy your creation!

INTERMEDIATE PROJECT

The following are five projects requiring intermediate tambour beading skills and the materials needed to complete them:

1. **Embroidered Handbag:**

Materials Needed:

- Fabric handbag or purse
- Tambour hook

- Beading thread
- Seed beads, bugle beads, or small beads
- Sequins or other embellishments
- Embroidery hoop (optional)
- Fabric glue
- Scissors

Step-by-Step:

1. Make sure your cloth purse is flat on the ground.
2. Securely knot the end of the beading thread after threading the tambour hook.
3. Choose a pattern for your purse, be it a geometric shape, abstract motif, or a floral pattern.
4. Dot the fabric with beads using the tambour hook in the pattern of your choice. To give your project more depth and texture, try using beads of varying sizes and varieties.
5. After finishing the beadwork, add sequins or other ornaments to the fabric using adhesive.
6. Make sure the adhesive is fully dry before you use your adorned purse.

2. Beaded Cuff Bracelet:

Materials Needed:

- Felt or fabric for the base
- Tambour hook
- Beading thread
- Seed beads, bugle beads, or small beads
- Larger beads or focal pieces (optional)
- Fabric glue
- Velcro or snap closure
- Scissors

Step-by-Step:

1. Measure the width and length of the fabric or felt strip you want to use for your cuff bracelet, then cut it to size.

2. Securely knot the end of the beading thread after threading the tambour hook.
3. Assemble the cloth strip according to your design by starting to thread beads onto it using the tambour hook. To make it more eye-catching, you might use bigger beads or focal points.
4. When the beadwork is finished, let the extra thread hang on the fabric's reverse side.
5. To make a cuff, glue the fabric strip's ends together.
6. To fasten the cuff around your wrist, attach a Velcro or snap clasp to its ends.
7. Your beaded cuff bracelet will be ready to wear after the adhesive has dried.

3. **Beaded Headband:**

Materials Needed:

- Fabric headband or hair accessory base
- Tambour hook
- Beading thread
- Seed beads, bugle beads, or small beads
- Sequins or other embellishments
- Fabric glue
- Scissors

Step-by-Step:

1. On a level surface, spread out your cloth headband or the base of your hair item.
2. Securely knot the end of the beading thread after threading the tambour hook.
3. Use the tambour hook to thread beads onto the fabric basis in a pattern or design of your choice. For a more dazzling effect, try switching up the beads and sequins.
4. When you're done beading, let the extra thread hang on the reverse side of the fabric.
5. If there are any beads or sequins that aren't already attached, glue them down.
6. Your beaded headband or hair accessory will be ready to wear after the adhesive

has dried entirely.

4. **Frame with Beadwork**:

Materials Needed:

- Plain wooden or metal picture frame
- Tambour hook
- Beading thread
- Seed beads, bugle beads, or small beads
- Sequins or other embellishments
- Fabric glue
- Paint or stain (optional)
- Paintbrush (if painting)

- Scissors

Step-by-Step:

1. After letting the picture frame dry entirely, paint or stain it if you like.
2. Securely knot the end of the beading thread after threading the tambour hook.
3. Use the tambour hook to thread beads onto the picture frame in a pattern or design of your choice. Either fill the whole frame or make a border around it.
4. Let the extra thread hang on the back of the frame after the beadwork is finished.
5. Adorn the frame with sequins or any other embellishments you like.
6. After the adhesive has dried, place a photo inside the beaded picture frame.

5. **Beaded Tea Light Holder:**

Materials Needed:

- Glass tea light holder
- Tambour hook
- Beading thread
- Seed beads, bugle beads, or small beads
- Sequins or other embellishments
- Fabric glue
- Tealight candle
- Scissors

Step-by-Step:

1. Make sure the glass tea light holder is clean and free of residue by cleaning it.
2. Securely knot the end of the beading thread after threading the tambour hook.
3. Using the tambour hook, start stitching beads onto the tea light holder's surface in a pattern or design of your choice. Beadwork bands around the top and bottom or the entire holder can be done.
4. After finishing the beadwork, let the extra thread hang on the back of the holder.
5. To make it more eye-catching, you can glue sequins or other decorations onto the holder.
6. Put a tealight inside the container and bask in the soft light of your beaded

masterpiece.

For beadworkers with a little expertise, these intermediate tambour beading projects are a great way to test the waters with more intricate designs and techniques. Make something truly special by playing around with various materials and patterns.

ADVANCED PROJECTS

The following are the materials and methods for three complex or advanced tambour beading projects:

1. **Beaded Evening Clutch:**

Materials Needed:

- Fabric for the clutch (satin, silk, or velvet)
- Tambour hook
- Beading thread
- Seed beads, bugle beads, crystals, or small beads
- Sequins, pearls, or other embellishments
- Fabric lining
- Magnetic snap closure
- Needle and thread
- Fabric glue
- Scissors

Step-by-Step:

1. Find the measurements of the clutch's body and lining, and cut two rectangles of cloth to those measurements.
2. With right sides facing, pin the fabric rectangles together and stitch all the way around, being sure to leave a little hole for turning.
3. Press the fabric flat after turning it right side out.
4. Securely knot the end of the beading thread after threading the tambour hook.
5. Use the tambour hook to stitch beads and ornaments onto the clutch surface, making a detailed design or pattern. You

have the option to decorate the whole surface or target particular regions.

6. Let the extra thread hang on the reverse side of the fabric after the beadwork is finished.
7. To improve the design, glue sequins or other embellishments onto the clutch.
8. Carefully sew the lining into the clutch, being careful to conceal any exposed edges.
9. Utilize a needle and thread to secure a magnetic snap closure to the upper edge of the clutch.
10. Your beaded evening clutch will be ready to use after the glue has dried fully.

2. **Beaded Statement Necklace:**

Materials Needed:

- Beading wire or jewelry cord
- Tambour hook
- Beading thread
- Seed beads, bugle beads, crystals, or small beads
- Larger beads or focal pieces
- Jewelry clasp
- Jump rings
- Needle-nose pliers
- Scissors

Step-by-Step:

1. Measure the length of the necklace you want to make and cut a piece of jewelry chain or beading wire accordingly.
2. Securely knot the end of the beading thread after threading the tambour hook.
3. Start making a beaded rope or chain by stitching beads onto the beading wire or cord with the tambour hook.
4. To add visual appeal and highlight certain areas, use larger beads or focal elements in the design.
5. Apply a jewelry clasp to both ends of the necklace using jump rings and needle-nose pliers when the beaded part is finished.
6. If you like, you can decorate the necklace with other dangling pieces.

7. Your beaded statement necklace will be ready to wear after the adhesive has dried.

3. **Wedding Veil with Beads**:

Materials Needed:

- Tulle or bridal illusion fabric
- Tambour hook
- Beading thread
- Seed beads, bugle beads, crystals, or small beads
- Sequins, pearls, or other embellishments
- Comb or headpiece
- Needle and thread

- Fabric glue
- Scissors

Step-by-Step:

1. Make sure the length of your veil is measured before cutting a piece of tulle or wedding illusion fabric.
2. Tie a comb or other headpiece to the veil by threading one end with a needle.
3. Use beading thread to thread the tambour hook and secure the end with a knot.
4. Using the tambour hook, thread beads and ornaments into the veil's surface to create a delicate and elaborate design. A delicate and sophisticated impression can be achieved by focusing on the veil's edges and corners.
5. When the beadwork is finished, let the extra thread hang on the fabric's reverse side.
6. To make the veil more beautiful, glue sequins or other decorations onto it.
7. Make sure the adhesive is fully dry before you put on your beaded wedding veil.

Create breathtaking, one-of-a-kind works of art that display your talents and workmanship with the help of these sophisticated tambour beading projects that provide room for originality and personalization. Putting elaborate beadwork and embellishments on your creations is a fun and rewarding process.

ADDING FINISHING TOUCH

You may take your tambour beading projects from lovely to spectacular by adding the final touches. For the last touches, consider these suggestions:

1. **Edge Finishing:**

   - Use a variety of techniques to finish the edges of your project neatly. You can fold the fabric over and stitch it down for a clean edge, or use decorative trims such as lace or ribbon to conceal raw edges.

2. **Embellishments:**

   - Consider adding additional embellishments such as rhinestones, pearls, or charms to enhance the overall look of your project. These can be glued onto the fabric or attached using small stitches for extra security.

3. **Lining:**

   - If your project requires a lining, choose a fabric that complements the colors and textures of your beadwork. Sew the lining into place neatly, ensuring that it doesn't detract from the beauty of the beading.

4. **Trimming Excess Threads:**

- Trim any excess threads from the back of your project once the beading is complete. Use sharp scissors to carefully snip away any stray threads, being careful not to cut through the stitches.

5. **Pressing:**

- Use a pressing cloth and a low heat setting on your iron to gently press your finished project. This will help to set the beads and flatten any wrinkles in the fabric, giving your project a polished appearance.

6. **Personalization:**

- Consider adding a personal touch to your project, such as initials, a date, or a special message embroidered in beads. This can turn your project into a cherished keepsake or a meaningful gift for someone special.

7. **Sealing:**

- If your project is likely to be handled frequently or exposed to moisture, consider sealing the beadwork with a clear fabric sealant. This will help to protect the beads from damage and ensure that your project stays looking beautiful for longer.

You can make sure your tambour beading projects last a long time and look great by paying close attention to these details. Enjoy the thrill of seeing your hard work come to fruition as you leisurely put the finishing touches!

Tips for Success

To help you succeed at tambour beading, here are a few pointers:

1. **Practice Patience:** Tambour beading can be intricate and time-consuming, so patience is key. Take your time with each stitch and bead placement to ensure precision and accuracy in your work.
2. **Start Simple:** If you're new to tambour beading, start with simpler projects and techniques before tackling more advanced designs. This will help you build your skills and confidence gradually.
3. **Use Quality Materials:** Invest in high-quality beads, threads, and fabrics for your projects. Quality materials will not

only enhance the appearance of your finished pieces but also make the beading process smoother and more enjoyable.

4. **Maintain Tension:** Consistent tension is crucial in tambour beading to ensure that beads are securely attached and stitches are uniform. Practice maintaining an even tension as you work, adjusting as needed to avoid loose or tight stitches.

5. **Experiment with Designs:** Don't be afraid to experiment with different designs, patterns, and color combinations. Tambour beading offers endless creative possibilities, so let your imagination soar and create unique pieces that reflect your personal style.

6. **Practice Technique:** Like any skill, tambour beading requires practice to master. Set aside regular time for practice sessions, focusing on refining your technique and trying out new stitches and beadwork patterns.

7. **Pay Attention to Detail:** Attention to detail is what sets exceptional tambour beadwork apart. Take the time to ensure that each stitch is neat and each bead is properly positioned, and don't overlook finishing touches like edging and embellishments.

8. **Learn from Mistakes:** Mistakes happen, especially when you're learning something new. Instead of getting discouraged, use mistakes as learning opportunities. Analyze what went wrong, make adjustments, and apply what you've learned to future projects.
9. **Seek Inspiration:** Draw inspiration from other tambour beading artists, historical designs, and nature. Explore different sources of inspiration to fuel your creativity and keep your passion for tambour beading alive.
10. **Enjoy the Process:** Above all, enjoy the process of tambour beading! It's a beautiful and meditative craft that allows you to express yourself creatively. Embrace the journey of creating something beautiful with your own hands and take pride in your accomplishments along the way.

Conclusion

Finally, tambour beading is an enthralling and satisfying art form that provides limitless room for individual expression. No matter how much or how little experience you have with beadwork, there is always more to discover and learn about tambour beading.

Stunning beadwork that reflects your talent and imagination is possible with practice, patience, and high-quality materials. If you want your tambour beading projects to turn out well, it's important to start small, try out different designs, and pay close attention to detail.

In the end, the satisfaction and excitement of creating something new is what matters most when tambour beading. Allow your creativity run wild as you bring your dreams of tambour beading to life; most importantly, enjoy the ride.

What you can achieve with tambour beading is quite remarkable; all it takes is perseverance, practice, and a little bit of inspiration. Have fun beading!

Printed in Great Britain
by Amazon

59924504R00040